LOUISIANA PURCHASE

DISCOVER

WESTWARD EXPANSION

An Educational Activity Book

S. PARKER

A special note to parents, grandparents, teachers, and friends:

Discover Westward Expansion is written for elementary school children. Educational information, participatory activities, and ideas are presented in an entertaining, light-hearted manner to encourage learning and creativity.

Jefferson National Expansion Memorial commemorates and retells the story of the westward expansion of the United States during the 1800's. The drama began with the Louisiana Purchase in 1803 and ended in 1890 when the Census Bureau declared an end to the western "frontier." The proud role St. Louis played during this time is symbolized by the magnificent Gateway Arch.

Written by Bobbi Salts
Illustrated by Steve Parker

Produced by American Educational Press
a division of Double B Publications
4113 North Longview
Phoenix, Arizona 85014

ISBN# 0-931056-03-9
Printed in the United States of America
Copyright © 1992 by Jefferson National Expansion Historical Association
11 North 4th Street
St. Louis, Missouri 63102
(800) 537-7962

TABLE OF CONTENTS

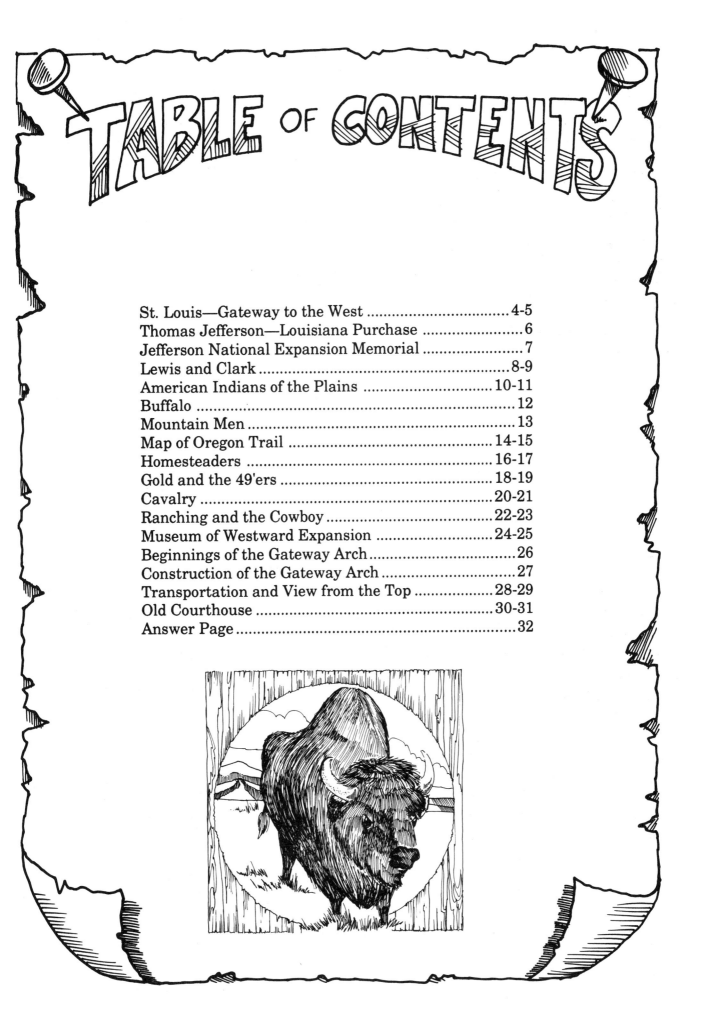

St. Louis—Gateway to the West

  St. Louis began as a small outpost in the wilderness in 1764 by trader Pierre La Clede. He chose a spot near where the Missouri River empties into the Mississippi River. He believed the Missouri River would be a major waterway for traders. He was correct! After America purchased the Louisiana Territory from the French, Lewis and Clark explored the new frontier from 1804 to 1806. Soon after this celebrated event, mountain men came to trade beaver pelts for a living. All major trails and paths led to and from St. Louis and it was not long before St. Louis became the gateway to the west!

  Today, we look upon this wondrous place and remember the important part St. Louis played in the westward expansion of our young country. The majestic Gateway Arch stands tall and proud as a memorial to the many people who passed by or through this gateway to open the vast wilderness for all.

4

Thomas Jefferson and the Louisiana Purchase

America's third president, Thomas Jefferson, had a vision. He could see our young nation stretching across the continent, from ocean to ocean.

During Mr. Jefferson's presidency, Napoleon Bonaparte, Emperor of France, offered to sell a huge tract of land to America. President Jefferson accepted Napoleon's proposal. On May 2, 1803, the Louisiana Purchase became official. Boundaries of the Louisiana Purchase extended from the Mississippi River, north from the Gulf of Mexico to the source of the Mississippi River and west to the Rocky Mountains. No one knew for sure, though, where the boundaries actually were, because no one had ever surveyed the land! The purchase price for the land was $15 million. That was approximately four cents per acre. The United States doubled in size! Without the vision of Thomas Jefferson, America would not be what it is today!

Jefferson National Expansion Memorial

The Jefferson National Expansion Memorial was created to honor the American explorers, trappers, traders, pioneers, soldiers, miners, missionaries, ranchers, American Indians, and others who made the lands west of the Mississippi a special place. Here at the Memorial, we retell the story of America's westward expansion. Without these people, there would be no story.

Today, the Gateway Arch proudly stands 630 feet tall and extends an invitation for all to pass by or through on their journey.

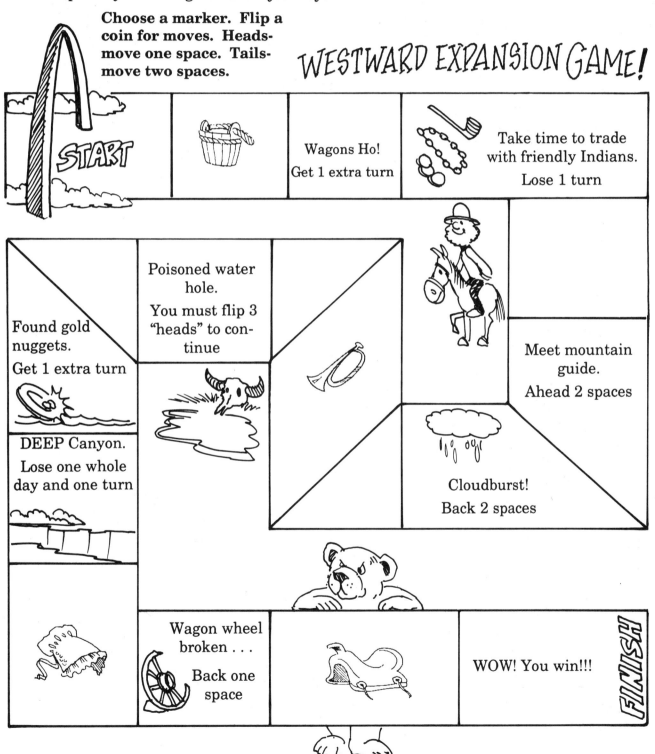

Choose a marker. Flip a coin for moves. Heads-move one space. Tails-move two spaces.

WESTWARD EXPANSION GAME!

START

Wagons Ho!

Get 1 extra turn

Take time to trade with friendly Indians.

Lose 1 turn

Found gold nuggets.

Get 1 extra turn

Poisoned water hole.

You must flip 3 "heads" to continue

Meet mountain guide.

Ahead 2 spaces

DEEP Canyon.

Lose one whole day and one turn

Cloudburst!

Back 2 spaces

Wagon wheel broken . . .

Back one space

WOW! You win!!!

FINISH

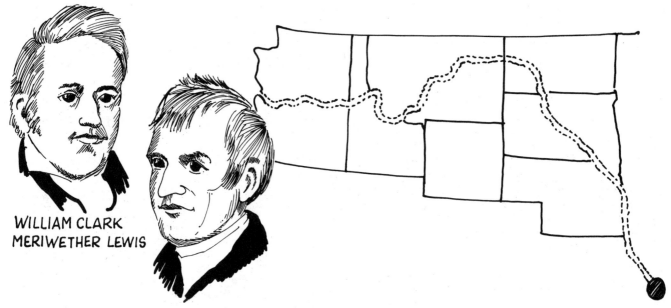

Lewis and Clark Expedition

President Thomas Jefferson sent Meriwether Lewis and William Clark on a journey through the new Louisiana Territory in 1804. Their mission was to explore and record their findings of the new land. The President was anxious to learn about the land he had just acquired. Jefferson directed Lewis and Clark to study the flora and fauna (plants and animals) of the Louisiana Purchase.

The expedition included Captains Lewis and Clark, 24 soldiers, a black slave (York), two interpreters of Indian languages, an Indian woman (Sacagawea), her infant son and Lewis' Newfoundland dog, Seaman. They left St. Louis on May 14, 1804. Items to be used for trade with the Indians included: Indian peace medals, red cloth, colored beads, scarves, calico ruffled skirts, jewelry, tobacco, and whiskey. Supplies for the expedition included: woolen overalls, hunting shirts, blankets, soap, saucepans, 193 lbs. of "portable soup" (condensed food), mills to grind corn, and guns.

Lewis and Clark studied minerals, hot springs, weather and soil conditions, as well as plants and animals of the new land. They discovered the pronghorn (which they called an antelope) and the grizzly bear. Lewis and Clark wrote detailed descriptions about their findings. Clark made detailed maps of the new land. Both men recorded their accounts in journals and sent records and collections to the President. Some items sent included a buffalo robe, bows and arrows, dried plants and roots, insects, animal and bird skins, a live prairie dog and a magpie.

The explorers began their journey on a keel-boat to navigate the river. At other times they used canoes. Sometimes they traveled by land (carrying their canoes), and sometimes on horseback or on foot. Lewis and Clark spent winters with the Indians and asked for their help throughout their journey. Without the Indians' help, the expedition would not have survived.

Lewis and Clark arrived in St. Louis two years after they began their journey on September 23, 1806. Their journals are some of the best records we have of the frontier years.

FIND YOUR WAY IN THE EXPLORER MAZE

American Indians of the Plains

Native Americans roamed the plains and prairies of North America for many centuries. A few tribes lived in permanent dwellings for a large part of the year, making their living by growing crops and hunting buffalo for food. However, most of the tribes adopted a mobile lifestyle, following the roaming herds of buffalo. The Native Americans hunted other animals, such as elk, deer, and antelope, but their main source of food was buffalo. The buffalo was sacred to the Plains Indians and their culture reflected the importance of this honored animal.

The Plains Indians lived in a movable home called a *tipi* which means "used for living" in Lakota language. Amazingly, the tipi could be assembled and taken down in about fifteen minutes. When the signal to break camp was given, the women removed the buffalo-skin walls and long poles of the tipi. The poles were harnessed to the side of a horse. A rawhide platform was formed which is called a travois (tra-VOY). Household belongings as well as children and elderly family members could be placed on the travois.

Find the two pictures in each row that match.

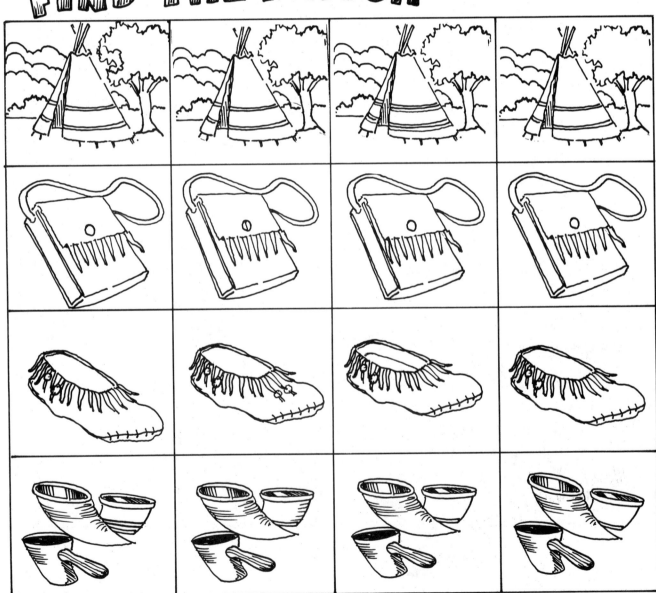

The buffalo provided much of the Indians' needs for survival. No part of the buffalo was wasted. All digestible parts were eaten and other portions were used for useful purposes. For example: buffalo hides were used for winter robes, caps, mittens, and leggings. Some hides were made waterproof and used for tipi walls, moccasins, pouches, purses, and saddlebags. Hooves were used to make glue. The fat was made into soap. Horns were used to make cups, ladles, and spoons. Ribs and the attached backbone were used to make toboggans for children during winter months. Buffalo hair was used to make ropes, ornaments, and leather balls. The stomachs were used as water jugs and the tails as flyswatters. And droppings were used for firewood.

The American Indians respected their natural environment. Every living thing was of importance to "the People," as they called themselves. Native Americans tried to live in harmony with their surroundings. Do you think people today respect nature? Do you think it is important to live in harmony with nature? Why?

Buffalo

About 1840, millions of buffalo, also known as American Bison, roamed the prairies and plains from the Mississippi River to the Rockies and from the Rio Grande to Canada.

For thousands of years Indians hunted buffalo without harming the numbers. The Indian believed there would always be many buffalo. Then the white man came. In the 1830's and 1840's buffalo tongue became a delicacy. The buffalo hide was used to make fashionable carriage robes and blankets. Hundreds of thousands of robes were shipped east. White hunters began killing more buffalo than the Indians. As more and more whites came, more and more buffalo were needlessly killed. Buffalo hunting became a popular sport for the white man. Railroads featured excursion trains through buffalo country so passengers could shoot the grazing herd as the train traveled. By the 1880's only a few hundred buffalo remained. The buffalo almost became extinct. The Plains Indian way of life was changed forever by the passing of the buffalo.

Preservation efforts forced Congress to pass a law in 1894 to protect the remaining buffalo. The "protected" herd, left roaming in Yellowstone National Park, had decreased to approximately 25 survivors! This law was the first effective measure passed by the government to protect the buffalo. Concerned citizens, led by William Hornaday, organized the American Bison Society. Hornaday lectured about the dwindling buffalo. The efforts of the Society saved the buffalo from extinction. Today, there are several protected herds and bison number more than 30 thousand! What an inspiration for all conservationists today, fighting to save other species from extinction.

Draw your own buffalo!

12

Mountain Men

When Lewis and Clark returned from their expedition in 1806, they reported seeing large numbers of beaver. Upon hearing the news, many adventurers chose to make their living trapping this plentiful animal. By the 1820's, the fur trade became big business for the many fur companies throughout the country. Beaver hats were quite fashionable in Europe and the eastern United States and the demand for beaver pelts was high.

Mountain men, as the trappers were called, had to deal with dangerous situations each day. Heat, cold, thirst, a grizzly or rattlesnake encounter, accidental drownings or gunshot wounds, and unfriendly Indians were a constant threat.

The mountain men met each summer at a predetermined place to exchange pelts for cash. During this meeting, or "rendezvous," the men would drink, gamble, fight, race horses, and tell "hair-raising" stories! After the two-week festivities, the mountain men would stock up with supplies for another year and head for the hills. However, by the 1840's, beaver was no longer in style and the once-abundant beaver supply had decreased. The trappers could no longer make a living trapping, so they turned to other means. Many mountain men retired to the Willamette Valley in Oregon Territory to farm. Others became guides to lead the many settlers across the frontier.

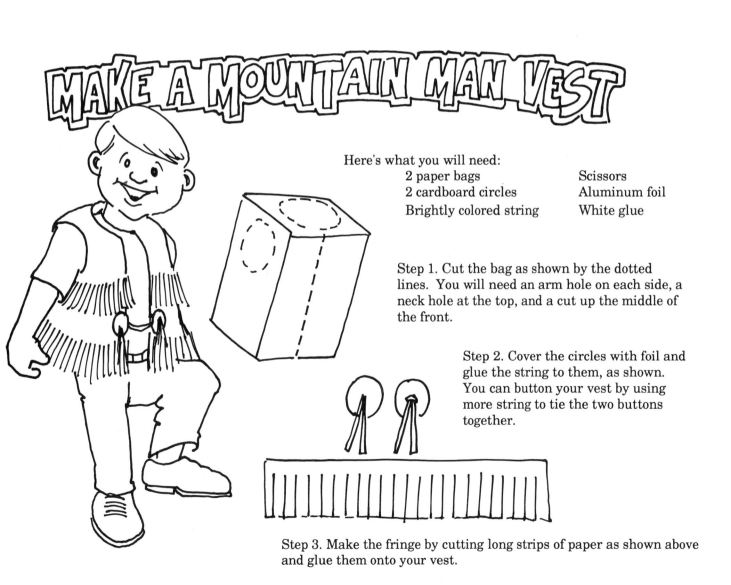

MAKE A MOUNTAIN MAN VEST

Here's what you will need:
- 2 paper bags
- 2 cardboard circles
- Brightly colored string
- Scissors
- Aluminum foil
- White glue

Step 1. Cut the bag as shown by the dotted lines. You will need an arm hole on each side, a neck hole at the top, and a cut up the middle of the front.

Step 2. Cover the circles with foil and glue the string to them, as shown. You can button your vest by using more string to tie the two buttons together.

Step 3. Make the fringe by cutting long strips of paper as shown above and glue them onto your vest.

Oregon Trail

The first long wagon train, numbering more than 1,000 settlers, left Missouri in 1843 and headed for the Oregon Territory. The long, hard journey of over 2,000 miles took six months to complete. Most of the settlers arrived safely and began farming in the new land. Thousands of people made this journey in following years.

Families packed their belongings in covered wagons for the long journey west. Farm equipment, household items, furniture, tools, flour, salt, cornmeal, coffee, and other necessary items were included. Some settlers even took cattle and horses to start their new farms. The trail wagon became a common means of transportation. The covered wagon measured about 25 feet long and had four wheels. Six or eight oxen were usually used to pull the wagon because they were strong and steady. At times, logs were tied to the wagon wheels to help keep wagons afloat when crossing rivers.

During the journey, the settlers faced hardships such as disease, drownings, accidental deaths, harsh weather conditions and other hazards. Many did not make it safely to Oregon, but the people who did complete the journey paved the way for future generations.

What are the ten most important items you would pack
for your trip to Oregon? Circle your choices.

Prairie Schooner

    St. Louis was a very busy place, especially in the spring. People gathered to share information, outfit themselves, and then board steamboats for Independence, Missouri. In Independence, the people formed wagon trains for their trip to Oregon. Some were disappointed when they arrived because stories they had been told were found to be exaggerated. But many more found they had traveled 2,000 miles to discover a rich land to cultivate and farm. Because of these pioneers, "Oregon Territory," made up of the present states of Oregon, Washington, Idaho, and portions of Wyoming and Montana, became part of the United States in 1846.

Homesteaders

The Homestead Act was signed by President Lincoln on May 20, 1862. The new law stated that a person was eligible to 160 FREE acres of farm land. The person who staked the claim would receive the deed to the land after the government was convinced the homesteader had lived and worked the land for five years.

After the Civil War, thousands of homesteaders poured into Iowa, Nebraska, and Kansas to stake out claims. Then they turned north to the Dakotas, and followed the railroads to Colorado, Wyoming, Montana, and Washington. It took just thirty short years to give away all the land suitable for farming.

THE "SODDY"

Because there were no trees on the prairie, homesteaders used the only material available—sod to build their houses. Chunks of sod were stacked to make the walls and roof of the home, called a "soddy." Can you imagine living in a house made of dirt?

The homesteaders faced many problems. Winter blizzards, summer duststorms, locusts, and drought drove some homesteaders away. However, many more stayed to endure the difficult times. These first prairie farmers were called "Sodbusters."

Find the ten things different in the two pictures of the "Soddy." Circle your answers.
You can check the answer page for the changes.

Gold and the 49'ers

  James Marshall discovered gold at Sutter's sawmill in 1848, near Coloma, California. The news of this event swept around the world, and within three months the gold rush had begun. Fortune-seekers from around the world traveled to California to chase their dreams and try their luck. Even the crews of clipper ships left their vessels abandoned in the San Francisco harbor and headed for the foothills of the Sierra Nevada.

  Thousands swarmed the California hills. The adventurers moved to other areas of the west as well. A few struck a rich gold vein, but many more did not. Most of the gold wealth ended in investment firms and big banks. John Marshall, the man who started it all, left the mining camps with no fortune of his own.

  The adventurers were called 49'ers, to mark the first major year of the California Gold Rush, 1849. The bearded prospector, his mule, gold pan, pick, and shovel symbolize these times.

Gold and the 49'ers

Discover the secret code. Find the correct letter that corresponds with the symbol shown. Check the answer page.

Cavalry

The cavalry had many functions in their role of opening the West. The soldiers explored and mapped mountains, deserts, and the plains. They also built roads, strung telegraph wire, guarded the railroads and stagecoaches, and protected the settlers from unfriendly Indians.

Find the hidden picture in the circle below. Shade the "X's" dark, and the "O's" light.

A soldier's life could be very lonely. After a day's work, the harmonica may have been a soldier's only companion. A married soldier may have been called away from his family and post for long periods of time.

When orders came to change assignments, the soldier packed all his belongings in large army chests and headed for new quarters and uncertain adventures.

CAVALRY COLOR PAGE

Ranching and the Cowboy

As the population of our country grew, the demand for more food increased and people wanted beef. The grassland prairie that once supported herds of buffalo could now support herds of cattle. Cattle ranching developed as a major livelihood. Cattle grazed freely on the open range land.

Men were hired to tend the cattle, round them up, and lead them to market. The cattle drive became a way of life, moving the herds across the prairie lands to the rail-roads in Kansas.

Find the hidden words. They are horizontal, diagonal, and vertical.

keelboat	buffalo	Lewis	ranch	plains
bison	homestead	Clark	oxen	beaver
soddy	Gateway	pioneer	Mississippi	grizzly
Napoleon	Missouri	tipi	Lakota	prairie schooner
cavalry	Jefferson	cowboy	elk	sodbusters

```
C R L U L X P W M O T B L I E Z R O W N
P O Z T A A K R U Z W I L Z M L E G J P
Q E W X R E K U M C X S P E S T O L V N
V F B B X J K O N A P O L E O N E R E N
L O K T O V R S T V A N L W D Z Z X L P
S W O D F Y L M N A V W X R D Z O O K T
P L R X L E N S T L X R Z N Y O O P R T
R L X A J E F F E R S O N S N I I P T Y
A A Y J S I W K L Y O X R S P L X I N T
I V N T S P O I N I X W R P L A I N S G
R S L C X O O P S I L E E I X R J V P G
I A S I H L M B U F F A L O R J D B B R
E B S J X M I Z Q U I L X N J R S L E I
S T O V R I S G T Q U X I E Z R T V T Z
C E D J M S L A V R S C E E P P A I L Z
H A B O S S I T J V R L A R V E I L X L
O B U S H O M E S T E A D L B V S T A Y
O T S B V U R W E I X R O N Z J G V I X
N Z T R E R W A J P P K E E L B O A T N
E S E J R I X Y E I O N L E R V J X P Z
R E R T Z O M L X V R I L T S V J L L T
L A S D N V M I S S I S S I P P I W R Z
```

22

Spanish explorer Francisco Vasquez de Coronado brought the first cattle into the U.S. to feed his men. The first cowboys were called *vaqueros*. Many words associated with the Old West have Spanish origins, such as lariat, ranch, and corral.

After the Civil War, the men hired to tend the cattle became known as "cowboys." This lonely job required a special person. The cowboy stood out as a rugged individual with a great deal of strength and courage.

A cowboy was known to stay in the saddle for 12-14 hours a day and most of that time was spent alone. Cowboys who tended the cattle at night had a difficult job keeping the herd quiet. Any sudden noise could start a stampede! The cowboys would sing soft, gentle lullabies to lull the cattle. Some of these cowboy ballads have been passed down to us. Others have been lost.

WHEN OUT ON THE PLAINS

Pretend you are tending a herd. What gentle lullaby would you sing to keep the cattle quiet?

Museum of Westward Expansion

Have you ever been to an underground museum? The Museum of Westward Expansion is built underground, below the Gateway Arch. The story of America's expansion westward during the years 1800 through 1900 is told here.

Exhibit areas display photographs, paintings, and things people said about the West. You can see stuffed animals such as a buffalo, longhorn, and beaver. An overland wagon, a steamboat's wheel, an Indian tipi, and the corner of a sod house are also displayed. You can see how the people lived, what they wore, and what they ate and said. You can see and learn about the great adventure of Westward Expansion.

Remember never to touch museum exhibits. Oils from your hands can harm the objects. Be sure not to step on exhibit platforms or feel the animals or prairie grasses. Keep in mind exhibits should be preserved for future generations to enjoy, too.

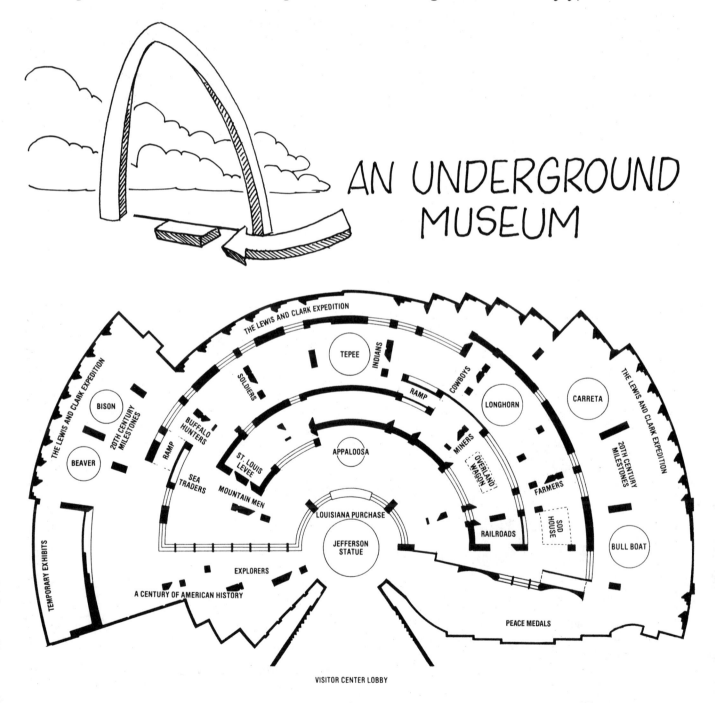

AN UNDERGROUND MUSEUM

The items below are hidden throughout the book.
Find each item and place the page number in the space provided.
Check the answer page for correct answers.

MUSEUM TREASURES

Beginnings of the Gateway Arch

A group of St. Louis civic leaders formed an association called the Jefferson National Expansion Memorial Association. Led by Luther Ely Smith, the association had an idea of building a memorial for Thomas Jefferson, the Louisiana Purchase, the expansion westward, and the role the city of St. Louis played during this time in history.

On December 22, 1935, the dream became a reality. President Franklin D. Roosevelt signed an order designating a 40-block site in downtown St. Louis as a unit of the National Park System. A memorial would be built!

An architectural contest was held to find a design for the new Memorial. Architects from around the country entered. In 1947, a man named Eero Saarinen won the contest. His design consisted of the 630 foot, stainless steel Gateway Arch.

Complete the mystery drawing. Find square #1 in the jumbled drawing. See how it is drawn in square #1. Now its your turn. Find square #2 and copy what you see. When you have finished all the squares, you will know the answer!

Construction of the Gateway Arch

When construction began on the Arch, the builders were faced with new problems. Never before had anything been built like the Arch. Very careful measuring was needed to construct it. One tiny mistake could cause the legs to fail to meet at the top!

The Gateway Arch is made of stainless steel, triangular-shaped panels which decrease in size as the Arch increases in height. When the last panel was hoisted into place, there was a two foot gap between each leg. The two foot opening was pried apart eight feet to slide the last triangular section into place. On October 28, 1965, the Arch construction was completed a little more than two years after the first section was placed. However, the underground visitors center, the Museum of Westward Expansion, and two transportation systems for the inside of the Arch were built later.

Gateway Arch Facts

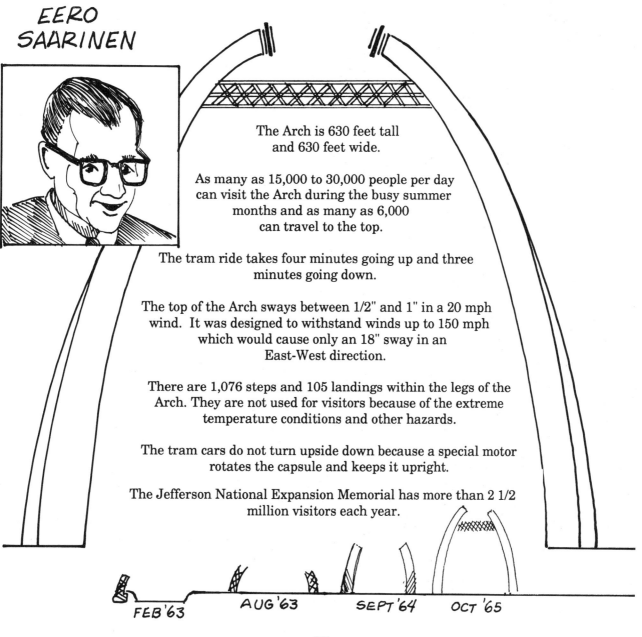

EERO SAARINEN

The Arch is 630 feet tall and 630 feet wide.

As many as 15,000 to 30,000 people per day can visit the Arch during the busy summer months and as many as 6,000 can travel to the top.

The tram ride takes four minutes going up and three minutes going down.

The top of the Arch sways between 1/2" and 1" in a 20 mph wind. It was designed to withstand winds up to 150 mph which would cause only an 18" sway in an East-West direction.

There are 1,076 steps and 105 landings within the legs of the Arch. They are not used for visitors because of the extreme temperature conditions and other hazards.

The tram cars do not turn upside down because a special motor rotates the capsule and keeps it upright.

The Jefferson National Expansion Memorial has more than 2 1/2 million visitors each year.

FEB '63   AUG '63   SEPT '64   OCT '65

Transportation and View from the Top

You can ride to the top of the Arch in a tram train! A transporter system carries visitors to the observation area at the top. A tram train with eight five-passenger capsules is in each leg of the Arch. The trams begin at the base of the Arch for the four-minute journey to the top. As the tram travels, it rotates to keep passengers in an upright position.

TAKE THE TRAM TO THE TOP

630'

305'

GATEWAY SPELLING QUIZ
"GATEWAY ARCH, A VIEW FROM THE TOP"

2 POINTS 3 LETTER

1. _____
2. _____
3. _____
4. _____
5. _____
6. _____
7. _____
8. _____
9. _____
10. _____
11. _____
12. _____
13. _____
14. _____
15. _____
16. _____

60 POINTS EXPLORER

3 POINTS 4 LETTER

1. _____
2. _____
3. _____
4. _____
5. _____
6. _____
7. _____
8. _____
9. _____
10. _____
11. _____
12. _____
13. _____
14. _____

How many three, four, and five letter words can you make from "Gateway Arch, A View from the Top"?

80 POINTS PIONEER

4 POINTS 5 LETTER

1. _____
2. _____
3. _____
4. _____
5. _____
6. _____
7. _____
8. _____
9. _____
10. _____
11. _____
12. _____
13. _____

100 POINTS '49 ER

Old Courthouse

The Old Courthouse stands high above the river in St. Louis. Now a part of the Jefferson National Expansion Memorial, it was once the center of community activity during Westward Expansion.

The Courthouse was built between 1839 and 1862. It served as a public meeting place for the citizens of St. Louis as well as a courthouse. Some of the Oregon-bound emigrants gathered and organized on the Courthouse steps. Today, you can visit restored courtrooms and museum exhibits on local and national history. The Memorial's headquarters are located here, too.

Before the Civil War, when Afro-Americans were held in slavery in the southern states, a very important trial was heard in St. Louis' Old Courthouse.

Dred Scott, a slave, sued for and received freedom. Another trial (an appeal to a higher court) ruled in favor of Dred Scott's owner—Dred Scott was returned to slavery. The case went to the Supreme Court for a final decision. The Supreme Court decided that Dred Scott should remain a slave. The results of this case made people in the northern states angry and hastened the start of the Civil War.

DRED SCOTT

Test yourself. Circle the correct answer. Check the answer page to see if you are right.

1. To quiet the herds at night, cowboys would...
a. sing songs b. build a fire c. rub the cow's ear

2. The Jefferson National Expansion Memorial Association was led by...
a. Eero Saarinen b. Thomas Jefferson c. Luther Ely Smith

3. Gold was discovered in California in 1848 by...
a. James Marshall b. Thomas Jefferson c. Marcus Whitman

4. Wagon trains going to the Oregon Territory had as many as...
a. 10 settlers b. 100 settlers c. 1,000 settlers

5. Wagons for the pioneers were called...
a. Chevrolets b. Prairie Schooners c. camper wagons

6. The Gateway Arch is more than...
a. 400 feet tall b. 500 feet tall c. 600 feet tall

7. The Plains Indians lived in a portable home called a...
a. tent b. condo c. tipi

8. The animal used by the Indians for much of their food and clothing was ...
a. buffalo b. elk c. oxen

9. The Gateway Arch was completed in...
a. 1963 b. 1964 c. 1965

Test yourself. Circle the correct answer. Check the answer page to see if you are right.

1. To quiet the herds at night, cowboys would...
(a.) sing songs b. build a fire c. rub the cow's ear

2. The Jefferson National Expansion Memorial Association was led by...
a. Eero Saarinen b. Thomas Jefferson (c.) Luther Ely Smith

3. Gold was discovered in California in 1848 by...
(a.) James Marshall b. Thomas Jefferson c. Marcus Whitman

4. Wagon trains going to the Oregon Territory had as many as...
a. 10 settlers b. 100 settlers (c.) 1,000 settlers

5. Wagons for the pioneers were called...
a. Chevrolets (b.) Prairie Schooners c. camper wagons

6. The Gateway Arch is more than...
a. 400 feet tall b. 500 feet tall (c.) 600 feet tall

7. The Plains Indians lived in a portable home called a...
a. tent b. condo (c.) tipi

8. The animal used by the Indians for much of their food and clothing was ...
(a.) buffalo b. elk c. oxen

9. The Gateway Arch was completed in...
a. 1963 b. 1964 (c.) 1965

Answer Page

FIND THE MATCH
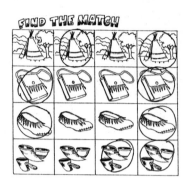

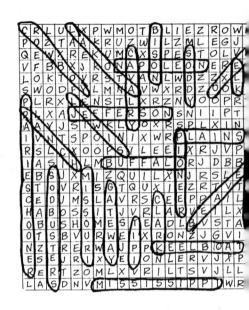

THE "GOODY"
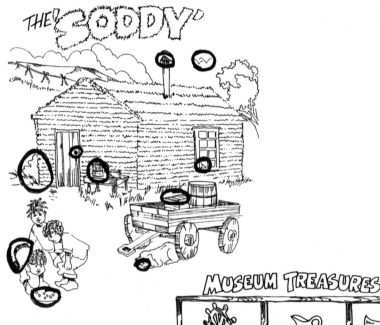

FIND YOUR WAY IN THE
EXPLORER MAZE

MUSEUM TREASURES